River Race

'River Race'
An original concept by Jenny Moore
© Jenny Moore 2022

Illustrated by Indira Muzbulakova

Published by MAVERICK ARTS PUBLISHING LTD

Studio 11, City Business Centre, 6 Brighton Road,

Horsham, West Sussex, RH13 5BB

© Maverick Arts Publishing Limited February 2022

+44 (0)1403 256941

A CIP catalogue record for this book is available at the British Library.

ISBN 978-1-84886-857-1

www.maverickbooks.co.uk

This book is rated as: Purple Band (Guided Reading)

River
Race

by Jenny Moore

illustrated by
Indira Muzbulakova

It was a sunny summer's day. Crowds of animals were waiting on the riverbank. They'd come to see the big river race – the most exciting event of the year.

RIVER RAC

4

Otter felt nervous as she did her warm-up exercises. She'd been training hard for weeks, pushing herself to swim faster and faster. She wanted to win the famous river race cup.

The other racers were getting ready too.

Duck was smoothing
her feathers with
her beak to make
them nice and
waterproof.

Frog was doing leg stretches
and jumps.

Water Vole was eating a pre-race grass snack,

and Beaver was floating in the water.

The crowds went quiet as Heron stepped up to the

start line. He was in charge of starting the race.

"Take your places everyone," Heron called.

"The river race is about to begin."

"Good luck everybody," said Otter as she joined

the others at the start line.

"Thank you," they said. "Good luck to you too."

Heron raised his long white wing, like a flag.

"On your marks," he called. "Get set... Go!"

They were off!

Otter shot away from the start line at top speed.

She could hear her friends and family cheering.

She was in the lead!

"Go Otter! You can do it!"

But wait, what was that? There was something

sticking out of the water ahead of her.

Otter tried to swerve but it was too late. Her front paw got caught in a rusty old bike wheel.

She was trapped! Oh no!

'Why would anyone throw a bike wheel in the river?' Otter thought crossly. She struggled to get free. How was she going to win the race now?

Otter wriggled and jiggled her paw. At last she let out a big sigh of relief. She was free. Phew!

Otter took the bike wheel over to the side of

the river, so no one else would get trapped in it.

She handed it to one of the helpers and then

got back to the race.

But she wasn't in the lead anymore... the other swimmers had all overtaken her. Poor Otter was right at the back in last place. She'd have to race harder than ever to catch up now.

"Keep going, Otter!" called her friends from the riverbank. "You can do it."

Otter swam faster and faster. She overtook Frog at the first bend and then shot past Duck.

Water Vole and Beaver were harder to catch but Otter didn't give up.

At last, she took the lead.

Yes!

Before she knew it, she was stuck again. Her back paw and tail were tangled tight in some netting, tugging her down under the water. Otter twisted and bit the netting with her sharp teeth.

But by the time she'd got herself free, Beaver and Water Vole had overtaken her. No, no, no!

By now, Otter was feeling cross and tired. But the race wasn't over yet. She thought about the winner's cup waiting for her at the finish line.

Otter swam harder than ever. Her tail swished in the water behind her. She kept a sharp lookout for rubbish as she drew level with Water Vole and Beaver – she couldn't afford to get tangled up again.

She dodged past another bit of netting and

a floating plastic bag. Phew, that was close.

At last, she was in the lead again!

There was the finish line just up ahead.

"Go Otter!" shouted the crowd.

"You're nearly there!"

Otter couldn't believe it. She was going to win!

But where were Beaver and Water Vole?
What had happened to them? Her heart sank
as she turned round to check.

"Help!" cried Water Vole
in fright. He was stuck in
some netting.

"Help!" shouted Beaver
from inside a plastic
bag. "I can't get out!"

Otter could see Frog and Duck behind them.

They were tangled up in

bits of rubbish

too.

The end of

the race was

so close, but Otter knew she had

to help the others. She forgot about winning

the cup and swam back to save them.

"Thank goodness!" gasped Water Vole as Otter freed her from the netting.

"Thank you!" panted Beaver as Otter pulled off the plastic bag.

Frog croaked happily as Otter set him free.

Duck couldn't stop quacking: "Thank you, thank you, thank you! I don't know what I'd have done if you hadn't come back."

Otter was too tired to keep racing after that, and so were the others.

"We think Otter should win the river race cup," they told Heron. "She was the fastest swimmer and she came back to save us. That makes her a double winner!"

The crowd cheered as Heron gave Otter the glittering river race cup. "Hooray for Otter!" "Thank you," she said. "And now I think we need a new race...

...a litter-collecting race to clear up the river and make it safe again. And this time everyone can join in. Whoever collects the most rubbish before the sun sets is the winner!"

"Great idea," agreed Heron.

"On your marks...

Get set...

Go!"

29

Quiz

1. What did Otter want to win?
a) The fastest swimming record
b) The blue ribbon
c) The river race cup

2. Who started the race?
a) Otter
b) Rabbit
c) Heron

3. What did Otter get her back paw and tail caught in?
a) A bike wheel
b) Netting
c) A tin can

4. What did Otter do when her friends were stuck in rubbish?
a) She carried on swimming
b) She went back to help them
c) She called one of the helpers

5. What new race did Otter suggest?
a) A litter-collecting race
b) An extra fast race
c) An obstacle course race

Book Bands for Guided Reading

The Institute of Education book banding system is a scale of colours that reflects the various levels of reading difficulty. The bands are assigned by taking into account the content, the language style, the layout and phonics. Word, phrase and sentence level work is also taken into consideration.

Maverick Early Readers are a bright, attractive range of books covering the pink to white bands. All of these books have been book banded for guided reading to the industry standard and edited by a leading educational consultant.

Pink
Red
Yellow
Blue
Green
Orange
Turquoise
Purple
Gold
White

To view the whole Maverick Readers scheme, visit our website at

www.maverickearlyreaders.com

Or scan the QR code above to view our scheme instantly!

Quiz Answers: 1c, 2c, 3b, 4b, 5a